These
Jeans
Aren't
Supposed
To
Be
Ripped

R M Brookes

These
Jeans
Aren't
Supposed
To
Be
Ripped

These jeans aren't supposed to be ripped

To anyone that'll listen,
And all those who understand,
You are not alone.

I hope you find comfort in these pages.

5

R M Brookes

Cover Design and Illustrations by R M Brookes.

ISBN-13:

978-1727457896

ISBN-10:

1727457897

These jeans aren't supposed to be ripped

R M Brookes

These jeans aren't supposed to be ripped

CONTENTS

ACKNOWLEDGEMENTS

Firstly I'd like to thank anyone who's picked up this book to read, however it was brought to you.

Thank you to my friends and family for being so loving and supportive, not only throughout this creation, but through everything.

To the one who spoke so passionately, believes in me and helped me put pen to paper.

For my inspiration behind the camera, who unfortunately will be unable to see what their inspiration has become.

My intention being, for you to live on in these pages.

A special thanks to you all

These jeans aren't supposed to be ripped

THE NAÏVE

These jeans aren't supposed to be ripped

PART ONE

THE NAÏVE

Personally,
The greatest language,
Is that of our eyes.

Meant for the old age
However born in the new

Views of mixed tapes and hand written letters
Replaced with keyboards and screen protectors

We were designed for a different life

Your eyes held galaxies
Infinite possibilities that took my mind
To ideas of what could be
Where mine held home
The calm amongst the storm at sea
They waited for you

Only you found home with another
Lips of burgundy
She's stained your neck
What was once mine is now lost to the wreck

The constellations that rest upon my body
The purples and pinks
Static lines down my consciousness like brush strokes
He sees a masterpiece on canvas
Slightly worn but every marking adding to it's value
I see a catastrophe
Now a story that in which can only be told
Only be appreciated when told by touch
The slow movement of his hand
Connecting the dots one by one

How easy it is to fall in love with the narrator
As they romanticise your imperfections

When you're near
I can't help
but mirror your smile

Be with someone,
Who's hello,
Becomes your favourite melody,
Voice, a song you must play on repeat.

How can we think clearly,
When we're looking at the world,
through filters.

His lies fall from his mouth
Like snow to the ground
Look for the truth in the eyes
It'll show like storms of sand

You think I wear these nails for them?
This is our protectionism,
Armour we've learnt not to leave behind.

You shouldn't be so easily fooled.

You let him in once.
You were used once.

He will lose you, once.

Once.

Dreams
are
a truth
we
won't let ourselves
believe

These jeans aren't supposed to be ripped

Coward
He keeps firing shots
Hoping I'll pull the pin from the grenade

Now I have you
I want another
Need him almost

How malicious
Is the mind
To make us crave
What we do not possess

We were chewing gum
That I had been using for too long
Taste turned flavourless
I needed to let you start a fresh

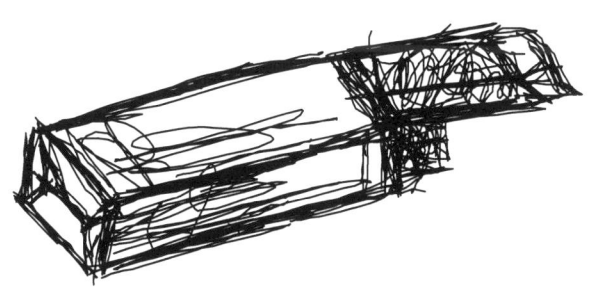

Alone
I am a masterpiece
Together
We are the whole damn exhibition

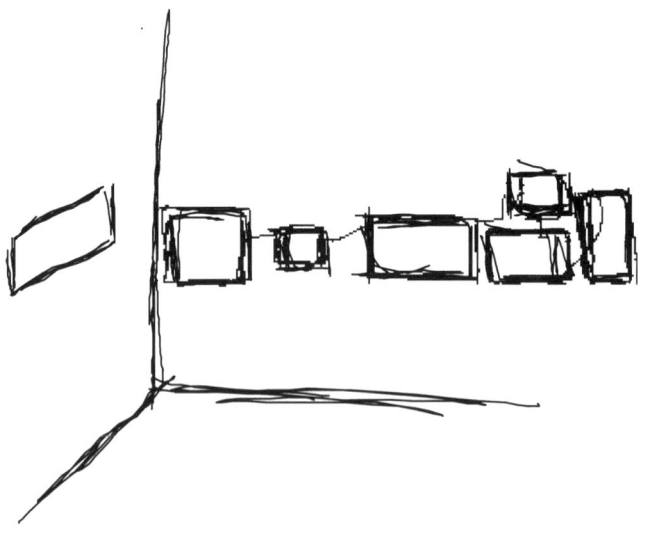

These jeans aren't supposed to be ripped

I've broken my own heart
for so long
Trying to find perfect

I completely forgot
How humbling
Being raw can be

She waited
Thirty two years
To get turned away
From her father

Again
History has a funny way
Of repeating itself
From time to time

I wanted
So badly
To fall in love with him
I prayed to a god
I never believed in
To begin with

Being biblical
Is no guarantee
Of purity and virtue

How evil you were
You showed me
A softer love
Safe and pure
Then proceeded
To shut the door
Leaving me
Out in the cold

Modern love

My 2am thoughts
Are made up of
Our late night matches
Of words with friends
Dreams of vowels
And how I can get the words
To rearrange
Confess myself
For a screen of brown eyes
I pray each game never ends

Girl

Don't give yourself away so easily
You never know when you'll need to hold yourself up
And how will you do that
When they're using you
To wipe their feet

It's not your heart that is the problem
It's the people you give it to
They don't know how to handle it

Remember
The scent of freshly cut grass
Rain on cracking soil
It's your favourite
Picking flowers and soaked clothes
And it suits you so well
Where it causes her teary eyes
And swelling throat
Sun pricked rash head to toe
With a stinging nose

He was to you
What the summer means to her

Loving you
Was like looking at the sunrise
Through the condensation
On the windows
Beautiful but not always clear

You're bluffing
When you say you love me

Call your bluff?
Maybe I will
I love you too
Emerald eyes and auburn hair
Makes my chest feel tight

Call your bluff
Green is now my favourite colour
You set my world
Into electric colours
You glow yellow when you smile at me

It is a dangerous game we're playing
I'm not sure if I've started call my own bluff
And I think I like that

He has taken my heart
And now I have nothing left for you
To which you reach into your chest
Offering me yours

This body has been mine
For twenty years
And now it listens to you
And I feel that I've betrayed myself

I stumble on words
Mutters and mumbles
Thought process on a loop
As it drags itself back to you

These jeans aren't supposed to be ripped

That smile of yours
Whispers lies in my ear
Makes me believe
That my right foot is my left

Out of date
A questionable choice
You drink me anyway
I'll be soft on the tongue
And fire in your throat

Wide eyed and lost
Take another sip
Glass laced with me
You'll soon get bored
They always do

I've always been
The Saturday night poison
Never the Sunday morning cure

Air

It's hard to believe that before you
I was starved of air
Left choked with empty lungs
For now, you are all that I breathe

~ when I say I can't live without you

Oh, Honey

Homemade honey
In makeshift jars
Elastic band seals

With handwritten labels
We were that authentic love
Real love that takes time

You can't buy this in store
Why rush something so delicate
Honey, take your time

Ours reminded me
That of fairy lights
We had a festivity to us
A notion to pick up and drop
You packed us away
And I wore us all year round
Maybe that's why in my eyes
We burned out to quickly

I think of us
With popping candy teeth
Taste of dust
Climbing haystacks in the wind
Dens of cloth
And why we ever stopped
Those where the best days
Even on the bad
We always did something
I miss our popping candy smiles

Growing pains

When the colour
Is absent
It gives a sense of distance
An ideal
Of simple pleasures
A perfect scenario
You'll know too well
Almost like
An old movie
Used once too many
Knowing the exact moment
It skips
Scratched appearance
Flickering where damaged
You know it's
Just a dream

When colour
Play it's part
It's almost like you
Are directly
In front of me
Blue smoke
From your cigarette
Flush of pink
In your cheeks
I get tricked from time to time
Wake up
Not knowing where
To turn
Who to look for
Wanting nobody if
It's not you

~ The advantages and disadvantages
of dreaming in black and white

Here I am
Stood at my window
Hustling myself
Into trusting you
I know I shouldn't
But I can be
so convincing

Why apologise to them
For thinking of yourself
You should apologise to yourself
For taking so long to do so

It's horrendous
The moment you realise
You've made a mistake
Like there's
A rock
The size of your fist
Lodged in your throat
It hurts to swallow
Catching your neck
On the sharp edges
Of your mistake
And when you're finally
Able to breathe again
It's bitter
Because now
It gets worse
Now
You have to admit
Your mistake

It's funny how you only know what you had. When you walk away and see it leaving you behind from a long distance. Too late to get it back. Just because you couldn't see what was in front of you the whole time. Now you've lost it all.
 - I was supposed to be the one to walk away, not you

Sometimes
The thought of you
Makes my chest rattle
As my heart
Becomes loose
In it's own cage

Look at what we have become
A montage of kisses
In bars in which the name
Has never stayed the same
One day relationships
Lost through lack of presence
These kisses always become
Texts hours apart
Meant to end
Within 24 hours

Give me something real

Ruin me

Leave me at 3a.m
Take that night from me
Make me miss you
Wrong me
So I sleep alone
Then come back

We'll do it all over again
And one day
This will ruin you.

It's you
I would've gone anywhere
Done anything
For you.

PART TWO
THE VULNERABLE

PART TWO

THE
VULNERABLE

His hand burnt my thigh
And with the absence of my voice
I lay motionless
Paralysed with every touch

Future intimacy
reduced to salt and ice

I didn't just light the match,
But drowned us in gasoline,
Lit the fireworks beside us and refused to run.

That soft beating heart,
Colossal drums on my chest,
Teeth shattering thuds.

These jeans aren't supposed to be ripped

Toxicity has a cruel way
Of disguising itself
from the human eye

I will bathe in bath salts and holy water
Before laying with you
But I fear
nothing will take away his touch
And how he's tainted
what was never his

It's how I've learnt
That when you say I love you
I ask,
For how long?

Deeply.
Hopelessly.
Endlessly.
When I love,
It's powerful,

Some might even say I'm addicted to self destruction.

These jeans aren't supposed to be ripped

I'm sorry
Sorry that my anxieties
Are such an inconvenience to you

Know you are okay,
Even if you're just okay,
Okay is enough.

I've always loved the rain
The sound as it hits the pavements
And the way it can be delicate to touch as it falls

And how it changes instantly
Soft puddles turn to vast lakes under your feet
Needles to the skin where thunderous roars meet the ears

I guess it reminds me of myself.

Next to him
Can be lonely
Being independent
Can be lonely

Sometimes
You can't escape lonely

He walked out
when she was old enough
To remember
But too young
To understand

Now she looks for him in everyone

I knew I'd lost myself
When I realised
He controlled me
With his looks

A 6a.m. wake up call
Stained sheets
The blood covered hands
Sore breasts
And burning stomach
Nothing compares to the panic
Disappointment in your inability
With bloodshot confirmation
It's the silence
When they ask you how you are
That sour look they give
Pitiful apologies
You go back to the bed
And stay there
Ignoring the world
Reminders of
Gender neutral yellow
He holds you
In tears
You know he feels like this too

Sponge

I'll be you're emotional sponge
Bring me your drunk confessions
Whiskey tears
Wine stained teeth
The porous coaster
To your feelings like water
Tell me your worries
I'll turn them to black coffee
Fix them for you
And soak up the spill
Earthy and strong
I'll give you a smile
My shoulder is yours
Sleep if you must
You'll not remember this
Once you wake
I'll add milk in the morning
Then you will share a smile with me

You will forget
You always do
I will remember
I remember every cup

These jeans aren't supposed to be ripped

I threw away my own voice
When I fell for his

And now I can't get it back

These jeans aren't supposed to be ripped

He saves me from
Blurry Saturday nights

Everything
Seems more solemn
At night

It is labelled arrogant
It is labelled ignorance
It is labelled clingy
Or too distant
It is labelled irritable
It is labelled weak
It is labelled immature
Or too childish
It is labelled overdramatic
It is labelled anger
It is labelled lies
Or too selfish

It's our disorders.
Our problem.

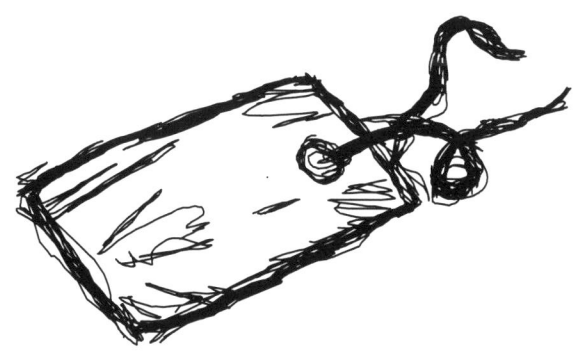

She tends to her wounds
With a simple smile
Soothes her past trauma
With reminders that she is worth more
Laces her memories of him
With softness and takes only the happy

Stop looking for reasons
As to why we are the way we are
The date and time
The deconstruction of our mental health occurred
I Believe the conversation
Involving depression and their friends
Is no longer getting cut short
Silenced
We are no longer getting silenced
But our voices
Grasp too prematurely
At the rope they've
Thrown to us
Or maybe it was their hesitation
That left us here
Still, we are here
And that is important

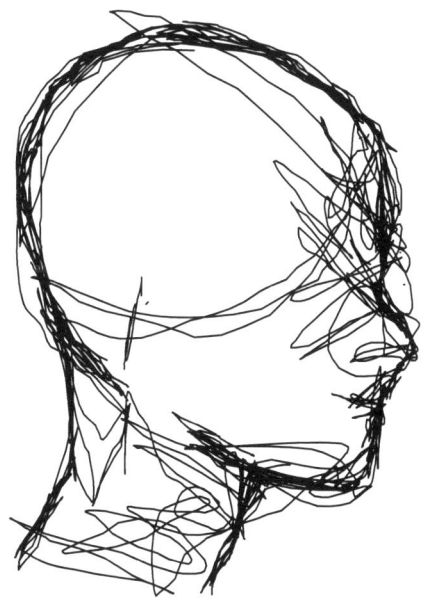

Stereotypes and expectations
Sexual Orientation
Is something to be found
Not told
It takes away the magic

They say jump into the deep end
That's how you learn to swim
But these water
Are not the same as yours
I'm swimming through the ocean
Yours a lake
You have a life jacket
And I'm carrying weights
You choose to dive on the count of three
I was pushed before I could breathe

I dare you to swim
In these currents

Only in the dark
He looked at me strange
Like feathers had replaced my words

Only when the lights are off
He smiled but shook his head
No one had argued before

Only when the lights can't reach me
Will I lay before you
Vulnerable and undressed

Only when it's light
I didn't come here for anything other
Than all of you

Only when the lights are on
Will we give ourselves
All we have

Only when the lights reach us
Will we see each other
For who we truly are

When I learnt of her
My body reacted like it had been locked in a sauna
When he spoke her name
My mouth had all moisture stolen
Made talking near impossible
Throat desperate for air
But the only air is too hot to inhale
Tastes burnt
Not something you want to take in
He goes on
But how could I concentrate

Walls caving in
My face must've been flushed
The heat near unbearable
He seemed fine
He was stood on the outside looking in
I wronged myself when I pleaded with him
Begged him to let me out
Slammed my hands to the door
Screamed at the glass
Burnt my fingers
Even my cheeks
Cracked lips and bleeding eyes
Who would love me after this

He had placed me here
Walked away with the key
Then gave it to her
I was never getting out

Cigarette burns
Only evidence
Of a father's
Drunken temper
Scars that'll
Last a lifetime
Motivation
To be
So much more
Than a result
Of looking
Too far back

Pieces

If we build ourselves
Out of what we find
When we break
For whatever reason
All you must do
Is pick up another piece
From our junk yard pathways
And if you cannot do that..

Well who says
We have to be complete
At all times

How could you bloom
When you're too busy
Trying to destroy others
From their roots

Desperate
I've known desperate
It's not longing for that boy
It's hunger
Stomach tearing itself in two
And giving your plate to your sister

It's knowing that if your foot
Slips from under you
You get no second chance
But you're walking a tightrope
And you're no circus act
You're human

Desperate is human.

Palpitations and murmurs
My heart creates it's own melody
Likes to catch me by surprise
Switches the blues
To heavy metal
On it's highest volume
Turns orchestra daydreams
Into clubland nightmares
Some days I pray for the piano keys

But when it's bad
The hyper rhythms
Still remind me that I'm alive.

Nightshift
Labourer
Seeing him leave our home
Like he was walking on hot coals
Return
With his mouth slightly upturned
A smirk of relief
But he returned weaker each day
A slow cracking
Monument of who he once was

When you've been so desperate for a certain kind of love. Obsessive. You look for it anywhere. Even in dangerous people. It's how something so pure can turn to toxicity so quickly. It's how being sentimental can become a harshest weakness.

At Night
When she turns off the lights
She's throws herself
Into the covers
Leaving only her head
Accessible to the cold air
Her lungs steal
A cool breath
Until it feels tight
In the chest
Heat becomes
Loose as it crosses
Her teeth

Begs her eyes
To adjust to the dark
Time to grow drowsy
Becomes
The point in which
She is most alert
Counting sheep
Becomes
An awakening
As silhouettes that once
Brought her nightmares
To life

Replaced with images of him
A memory more haunting
Than monsters and demons
What a reputation
You have built
How many others
Fear you
At Night?

I take control
By breaking my own heart
More times than anyone else can

I refuse to give them the chance
I refuse

Each time you embrace me
This shield is popped
Damaging my bubble wrap armour
I've built it around this body
And mind
To protect myself
From people like you
Each time it becomes
More useless
One day you will get to me
I'm already powerless to you
Still you crave the control
I shouldn't have fell
Into this possession
Dressed in thorns
I'm yours for life
Damsel caught by the tyrant

THE HIDDEN

These jeans aren't supposed to be ripped

THE HIDDEN

Once they ask you to pick,
Chose the bitter smoke,
The tar filled lungs,
That five minute break in those endless shifts,
The aroma of self infliction lingers,
As does the addictive cough that's maturing with every breath.
A blue cloud formed for your immediate vision.

Never the champagne,
The bubbles that whisper congratulations
The fizzing that puts most into a translucent state.
That obnoxious clinking of their finest glasses.
What's there to celebrate?
No more self obsessed anecdotes dripping off the tongues of the superior,
Or canned laughter send teeth on edge everywhere. Distinctively lower the glass,
It's a silent revolution.

These jeans aren't supposed to be ripped

If I were bitter,
I'd say,
I hope my happiness hurts like
A wasp sting to the
Throat.

These jeans aren't supposed to be ripped

When will it stop?
Hearing you in all my favourite songs?

I'll train my words
To fall like sunflowers
When I talk of you

Although I'm sure
Those you speak of me
Won't survive the height

The discomfort is
Temporary,
The achievement will be
Permanent.

Excuse my self indulgent tongue
By you've made your bed
My love could've eclipsed hers
But at least I've had a swift getaway

His being
rattled around in me
like a lost spirit,
Presence
of an unwanted visitor
molded from my distress.

And somehow
Doing nothing
Became better
Than trying, just to fail

Poison

Typically a substance
Preserved to cause harm
Meant to take over the body
Unfriendly and aiming to mutate

My body has been taken
I never thought
That my poison
Would turn out to be myself

When did I become the villain
To my own mind?

Jesse
They've changed the doors.
It was broken and unsafe but,
How dare they rip out what was once yours.
Taken the leather and thrown it to the flames ,
Books drowned in home made wine.
Every creation,
Turned to nothing but firewood.

The only thing that keeps you alive,
To me,
Are in those walls.
But it was never within the bricks.
Never the furniture cementing your existence.
But in us,
These hands that look like yours.
The way I put pen to paper and photograph the earth.

Watch over me,
Help me take a deep breath and start again.
You were the one,
You taught me how it felt to have someone stand behind me,
Felt the pain of the knife before it reached my back.
But now you're gone and I'm,
I'm completely exposed.

Arguments around us,
Fell like shrapnel on our skin,
But you told me that whatever happens you'd be by my side.
I am struggling,
In a world I don't belong in.
You managed,
You did it so well.
And how you said we were your legacy,

Surprise,
But I don't feel worthy of that name.

Even when they shuddered the word terminal,
I did not cry.
I threw myself into notebooks.
Made it my mission to keep you alive through words.
I never did succeed.
You still left.

One day I will learn
Learn to except the help I need so much

Today is not that day
Today I lock the doors and pretend I'm not home
I'm not ready to part with my stubbornness

Being the best
at second place,
Has become
a common pastime.

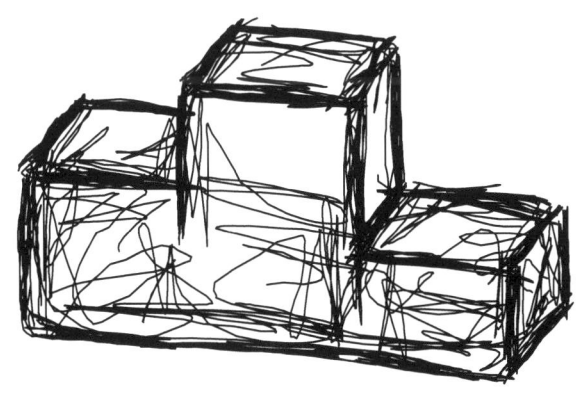

5a.m

Looking down the street whilst intoxicated
Soaking up the first sight of the sun
Before losing the battle with slumber

Waking up for those early starts
Sipping orange juice with bits and eyes closed
Desperately holding onto the dark before becoming fully alert

It's a bittersweet time

His scent
Clings
To my clothes
Fabrics
His last
Cruel joke
Where I appear
To be yet another punchline

Being yourself
In a world
That doesn't want
You to be just that
Is achievement enough

Tonight I'll create
A different type of art
Paint myself in
"I love you"
And red lips to his collar
Designed revenge
For all of my sisters
This piece will be monumental
It will even take
His icy breath away

Eating breakfast
Keeping breakfast down
Facing the mirror
Facing family
Starting a family
Grief
Religion
Doctors appointment
Hospital Treatment
Covering the bruises
Cuts and scars
Stepping out the house
Getting out of bed
Saying hello

Invisible battles
Are still battles

These jeans aren't supposed to be ripped

I'm ashamed to say
I've found comfort in the winter
Cold nights
forcing early retreats

Using superglue
To attach the chipped pieces
From where I've been crushed
By his careless hands

She is healing
It's a new kind of fight
And she's winning

You will allow your heart to grow

Not by the side of a man

Who neglects to tend to it

But in the arms of yourself

I want broken glass at 3a.m
Your insults
My stubbornness
I want tear stained faces
And late apologies
Battles for the last words
I want the house to know
Slammed doors
And cold dinner
I want us in dim light
Insecurities shown
Both of us flawed
I want it all
Every raging moment
And all consequences left for morning
Give me all of you
Dark and light
The whole colour spectrum In-between
I'd rather fight through the night
Pillows ripped
Feather covered floor
Than for you to leave out that door

On the good days:
Give me an early start
One alarm will do
Can I take your order?
Work is no problem
I'll buy that set of lace underwear
The ones that are a little,
You know?
Those days mean
Let me help you with that.
Hey, I haven't seen you in a while
Did you want to meet up?
Damm, you are incredible girl
Late night adventures
Drinks, drinks and maybe more
It's safe to get a little drunk
On the good days
Give me the world

On the bad days:
What's that buzzing
I'm not leaving this bed
Forget about the front door
Greasy hair with a side of blemishes
Let's stare at the mirror
11 unread messages
Great, aches and pains
Can't face work
Unhealthy Instagram comparisons
I'm sure t.v. will help
It'll be a distraction
Oh, they need help with that thing..
That's a lot of apologies to make
Can't make today
The bad days
Must hide the liquor
I want to leave this world

These jeans aren't supposed to be ripped

Today
Is an acoustic indie playlist
Type of day

She finds him in moments
She wishes she didn't

He follows her to the coffee house
The smell of freshly ground coffee beans
Reminders of his order
Black, no sugar

She's not over him yet
But one day
She'll walk into that coffee shop
And that scent will mean

    Just another cup of coffee

Shared books
With broken spines
Vintage horror movie
We learnt all lines
Watched them again and again
Until we damaged the discs
Late night cartoons
making pumpkin pie

You're my charity shop sister
With rainy beaches
And early morning walks
Getting caught in the seaweed
You'll visit most my stories
I still wait for the day
You knock on my door
It's been so long

I pray I'd be brave and answer

Getting over you was a skill
One I practiced too much
But couldn't properly master
Like learning the guitar
I had painful reminders

Blistered fingers
From holding on for too long

All the drugs
The alcohol
Even the sex
It only masks
After it all fades
It comes back
Back to a feeling
That never truly clears

We all know that really

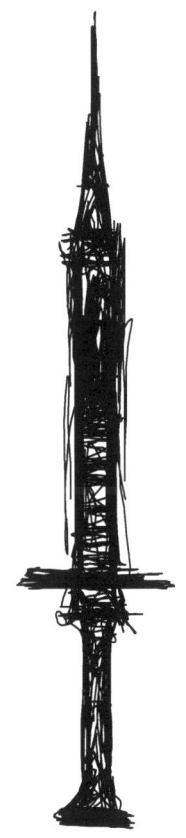

How melodic
It was as he danced
On my body
Silk to the skin
Steps I'd only dreamt
Movement like water
Warm breath to cold air
Sweet tongued
And hands of clay
He molded me
Arched chest
I noticed only
His shoulder blades
Tearing himself at the seams

Fingers and toes clench
With handfuls of feathers
Lips bitten from dry teeth
How I'd held on to the notion
No man like him
Could intertwine with a woman like me
Proved wrong
With grazed knees
And glazed eyes
Someone waited for me
And I didn't cower
But followed
At my own pace
I've now found my place

An amazing ability
Of not knowing when
To hold my tongue

I swear my voice
Would fight through clenched teeth
To free itself

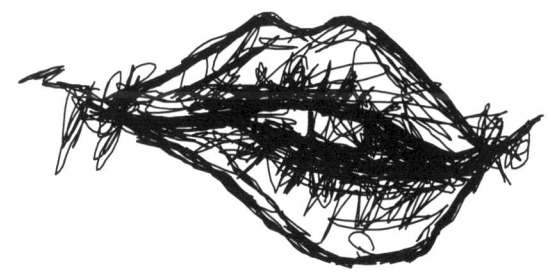

Sometimes
Some days
I neglect
To show myself
Kindness
I save it
For those nights
The ones
That put
everything
Into perspective

When we need it the most

I try to stray
From jealousy
And begrudgeny
But you always
Take me back

...

As a woman
refuse to be concealed
Call yourself controversy
Do not apologise
For being alive
Tell them
To turn the other cheek
If they must
Pity their ignorance
They don't deserve you

~ A message to their daughter

Fingertips

At night
When our little town is asleep
There's only the faint sound
Of cars in the distance
I think of you

In the mornings
When my mind is still quiet
Too early for light
I'm reminded
Of the subtle touch
Of your fingertips
Tracing my back

It seems so vivid
If it's quiet enough
I'll feel your fingertips move
Glide down the side of my cheek
If it's dark enough
You'll miraculously appear
In front of me

At night
When our little town is asleep
There's only the faint sound
Of cars in the distance
I think of you

Dive into the pages
Be an emotional refuge
Hide amongst fables

We were like
A novel that someone
Couldn't find interest in
We would get picked up
Our story would move
We would already know every word
On each page turned
Anticipating every line
Then the bookmark would appear
We never knew next time
We'd get picked up again

Sad that we couldn't control
Our own story
That it was left to those
Who did not care

Side affects as stated

Feeling like an unfinished puzzle
Constant need to fill an uncompromised void
It refuses to be filled
Detachment comes in flashes
Overactive imagination
Feeling like a glass of water
Half empty
Seeing yourself
As part colour
Part black and white
Desperate need for approval
Often deep longing
To search for what you never had
But known was always missing

~ the side affects of the absent father
They will always be better, than he could ever be

It's not that I'm aging
Or considered alone
It's not that time is running out
For me to provide a descendant
Why would I be so selfish
When there are children
Already alone
Looking for a home
I will be a home to many
Not just the few
Just because of genetics
It's an easy option I refuse to take
I'll take the rough country roads
Make connections
With those who's had their own
Burnt away
They will be my children
And I'll meet them everywhere
I turn.

Is it bad?
To desire a sober love
Love that doesn't
Demand a percentage
To be real?

Sad to say
Recently
The only affirmations
We've seen past 12am
Off of boys
Playing heartbreakers
Are dick pics
And nude favours

Eventually
There will be men who
send their hands
Sew together the holes
Where youth
Broke our chests wide open
And allowed the world
To take what it liked

PART FOUR

THE CLEANSED

These jeans aren't supposed to be ripped

PART FOUR

THE CLEANSED

Humanist
    What that basically means is
    I've trained my tongue to feel like sandpaper
    When I talk of faith

My scars are now
Just victories of yesterday
Mapped out on my body
Like stories of bravery

You fuchsia nailed hurricane
You sharp tongued, glittery goddess
Because that's how you survive
Forget those looking at the world in black and white
Pity them
They miss the rainbows
Sun breaking through the clouds on a rainy day
But you are the light
You warrior in lip-gloss
Take those heels to the dirt if you must
Stamp out the dated views with stilettos
You lone wolf
Turned royalty
Mighty hair and eyeshadow war paint

Promise,
You'll lead this show?

These jeans aren't supposed to be ripped

If lessons in life
were easy,
These pages
would be bare.

Putting pen to paper

    Has become as easy

        As taking a deep breath
          First thing in the morning

When I first wore make-up
I was met with patronising words
When I stopped wearing the mask
I was met with silence

That meant more
than a hundred pin pricked smiles

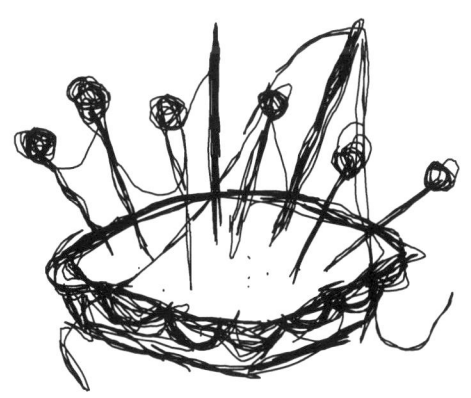

I sing, not to be heard
I dance not to be seen
I love, not for you

But for me, it's all for me

.

I'd rather stain my arms
With roses of ink
Than receive plants plucked from the earth
Tied with your lies

Late talks
Cheap haze
Drunken smoke
Street lights to sunrise

Country roads
Windows down
Cliché music
Backseat company

Lost moments

Don't allow yourself
to feel trapped
by where you've came,
It does not control
your next move
in the game.

We are born alone
So we can become
Our own heroes

I've slowly fallen in love
With the way my hair falls over my face in the mornings
Both messy and Authentic
I no longer begrudge my natural hair
The way the colours come back
Looks silver and grey compared to its imposter
Waves and kinks that stand strong and stubborn against the heat

A strength I aim to match.

Tonight I submerge myself
Into bathwater and sage
Conduct an exorcism
Of my own

Dive into the memories
Of you
Drive them out
They've overstayed their welcome.

When did my kindness
Get confused for weakness
I must remind myself
It's a strength they will never have

It's an unusual sensation
Regaining your strength
I returned stronger
Than when I left

I'm not kept awake
Worrying about how I'll meet
"Prince Charming"
Why would I need a boy
I was already born a damn Queen

The strongest of us
Are those who have been broken
We know you can rise
After the fall

Your mental health does not make you less of a person
It makes you stronger than most
Some just choose to ignore that detail
That means sometimes you're overlooked
Do not let that discourage you
You are fighting your battles
In the mornings
Before they've even had their first cup of coffee
That takes guts

You are only human
Be human

When I think of you
I begin to feel flies in my mind
You've been there too long
You've begun to rot

They only return for you
You must leave now
I will not carry this rubbish
I've placed you in a black bag

And tied it up
Ready to ditch you
Where you belong
You will not drag me with you

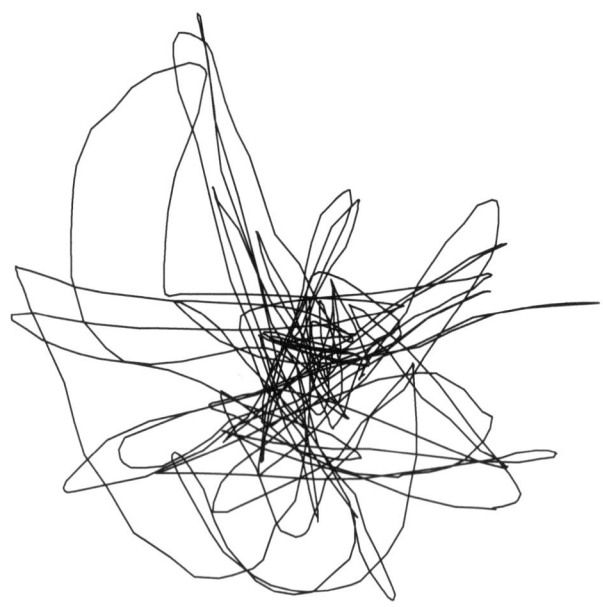

Is that dirt
Greasy hands
Filth under the fingernails
Get me to the sink
Let me wash my hands
Soapy heaven
Boil the water
Burn these fingertips
I cannot keep this on me
Not a second longer
Perhaps a shower will shift this
Steam this body
Rub the grime off of my skin
You will not live with me anymore
Even if I must burn you out
I will be cleansed

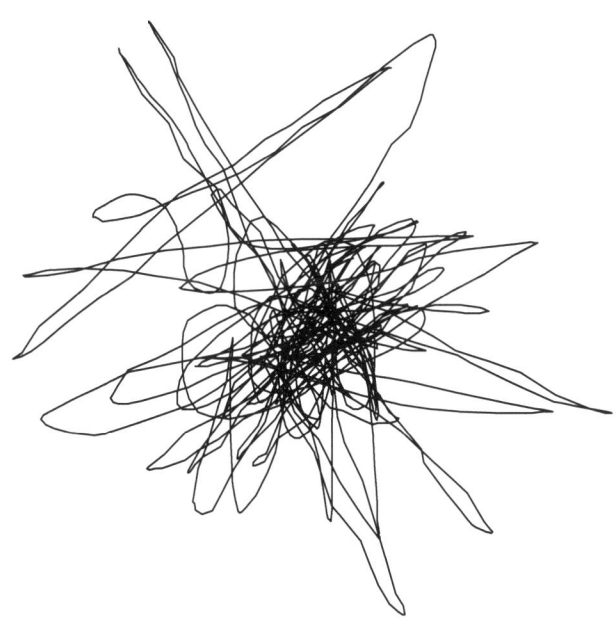

Lullaby

Be your own savior
The one who sings you to sleep
Wakes you up with a smile
Clears your completion
And complements it all day
Gives you composure
In the chaos of your day
And carries you body back to bed
When it's completely necessary

Be your own lullaby

Someone new
Is not your way out
It is you

Toothpaste
I crave your spearmint lips
Soft bristles on the gums
Mouth cleansed
Our toothpaste night
Just a peppermint dream
These teeth will be stripped
Before meeting with you

Cold Water

I've decided to change
My relationship with water
Previously it has been abusive
How could I treat
Something that gives me life
With such blindness

I'm pouring myself
A glass of cold water
Drinking the whole cup
And I shall thank it afterwards
Then collect more with my hands
Wash today off my face

Delicate
Our fragile skin
Take the words
Of lesser minds
Paints them upon us
Like branding
To which we say
We shall wear them
Like part of us
Leaving these mere words
Useless
Compared to our
Body language
Which screams
The opposition
How dare you label
Something so unique

In those pictures
I exaggerate my collar bones
Use make-up to create illusions
Chisel and reconstruct
Without it all
I still love myself
Round face and red cheeks
Pale skin and freckled nose

Love every version of yourself
Either way it's one in a million
Because it's all you
No one else has that

Admitting you're flawed
In a world that demands
Perfection

~ is still bravery

These jeans aren't supposed to be ripped

We're surviving
But only in part
It's time for living

Last words

I hope it soothed you
Recalling your DIY successes
Our homemade Wendy house
All yours
A granddaughters safe haven

How you'd lean inside
Barely fit your torso
You'd cut out the windows
Replaced with tee towel curtains
Once our favourite place

It lay in the garage
gathering dust
But you never discarded it
I hope it gave you peace
The last memory you relived

You had given us
So much more
Than a simple Wendy house

Tonight I am back
There will be no
Ice cream salvation
No rom-com tears
Or sofa daydreams
Clichés, blankets and sweats
They're all banned

Tonight I'm painting
Myself pretty
Wearing my favourite outfit
The one you hated
Pouring a glass
Or two
Either way I'll decide

Tonight
You walked out
But I'm stepping up

We are the healer
Looking for the broken
Collecting them
Like souvenirs
Hung over the fireplace
Like congratulations
On your achievement
It is not our
Standing ovation
Our companions

But I remind you
To see the broken
And stand beside them
You must have known broken

These pages stay bare
The right words evade me
I swear it's because of you

There's no happy memories
No painful recollection
Just because you survive

- to the bad parts of me, I'm leaving you behind

I'd lived before you
I've lived through you
I'll live after you

Have you ever looked
At a bruised peach
It appears delicate
Softened from the hit
Perhaps with
slight discoloration
On the skin

You left me
Like you dropped
A piece of fruit
Wasted on the floor
I remind you
It doesn't affect
my sweetness

Ear to your chest
Immediate sanctuary
Your heartbeat slowing
And somehow reaches mine

Can't wait
for the woman I'm becoming
I'm fighting for her
Everyday
Because she's
Who'll take on the world

To expect the world
And give nothing
Is to receive less

To leave expectation
And give all you have
Will bring the universe

I
was
only
ever
mine,

It
just
took
you
for
me
to
see
that.

THE AUTHOR

Social Media

Instagram: @dr.watson98_
Twitter: dr.watson98_

Dear Reader,

Thank you so much! I applaud anyone who has made it this far and am thankful that you've chosen to do so. It means so much that you'd take the time to read these words.

It is terrifying to put something so personal into syllables and print it. Therefore, I'm so sorry to anybody who has understood some of the works in this collection. Take care with this creation. It is here for anybody that may need it, and me speaking through pages.

These jeans aren't supposed to be ripped

When there's no one around to show kindness
Be kind to yourself

These jeans aren't supposed to be ripped

27057429R00111

Printed in Great Britain
by Amazon